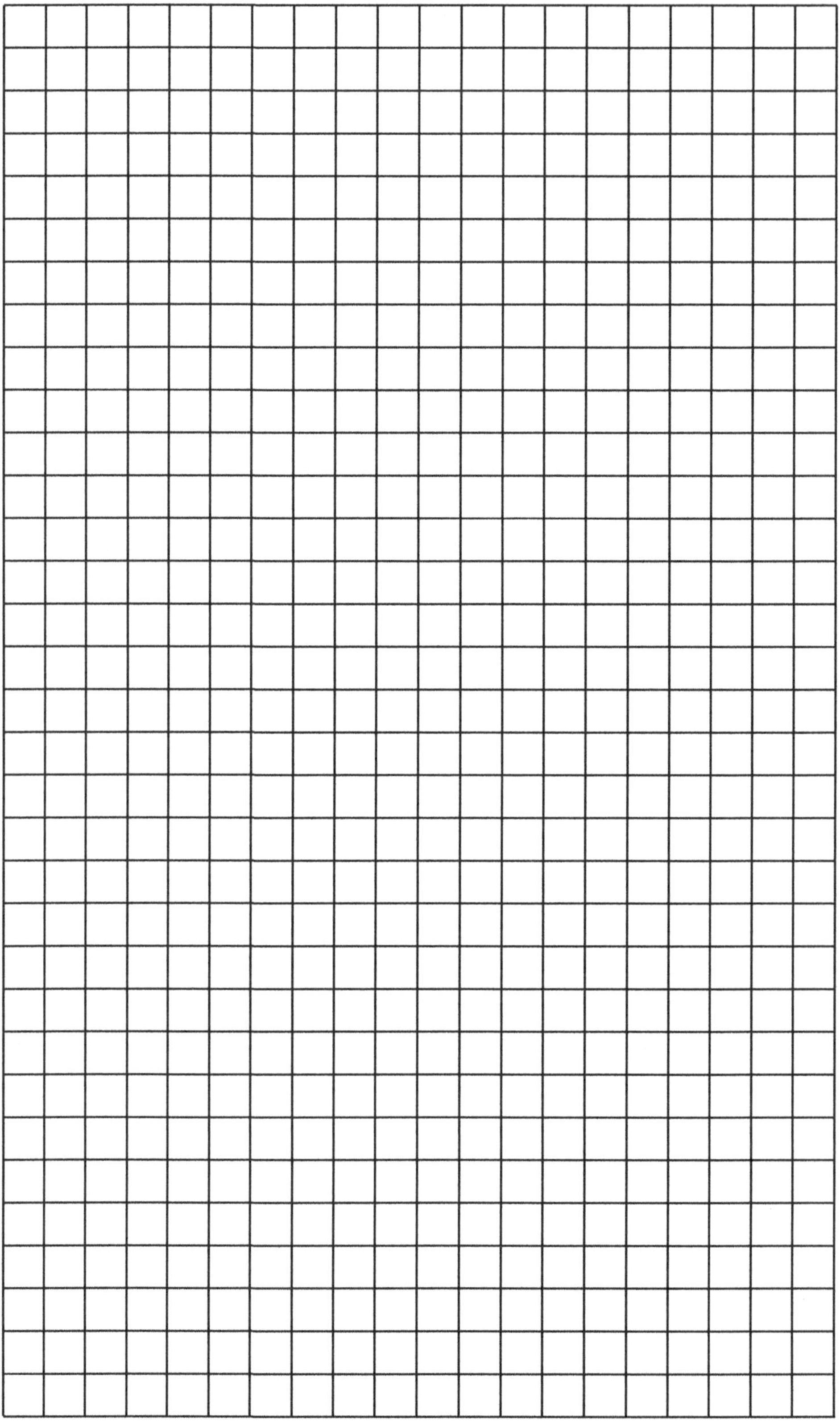

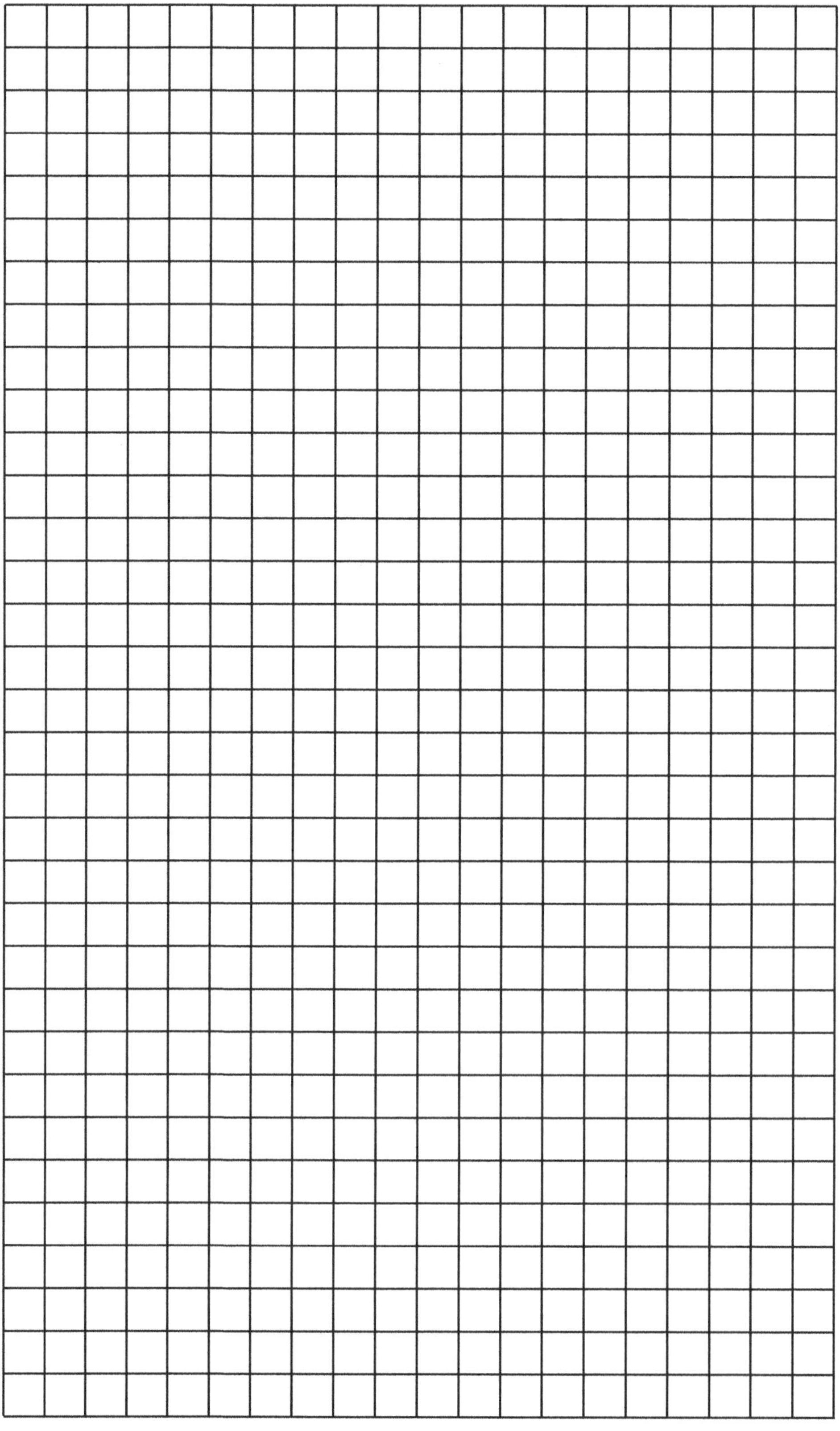

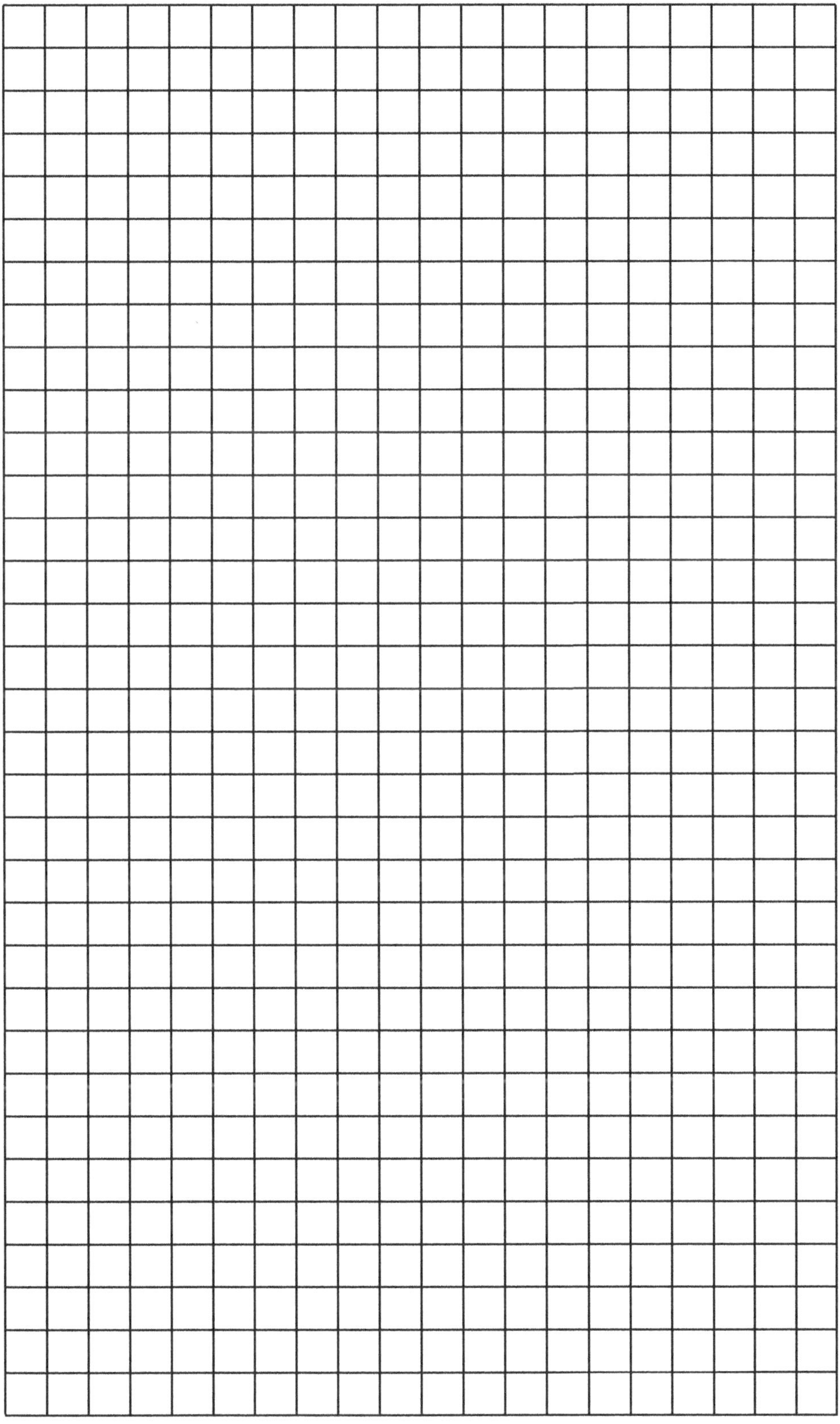

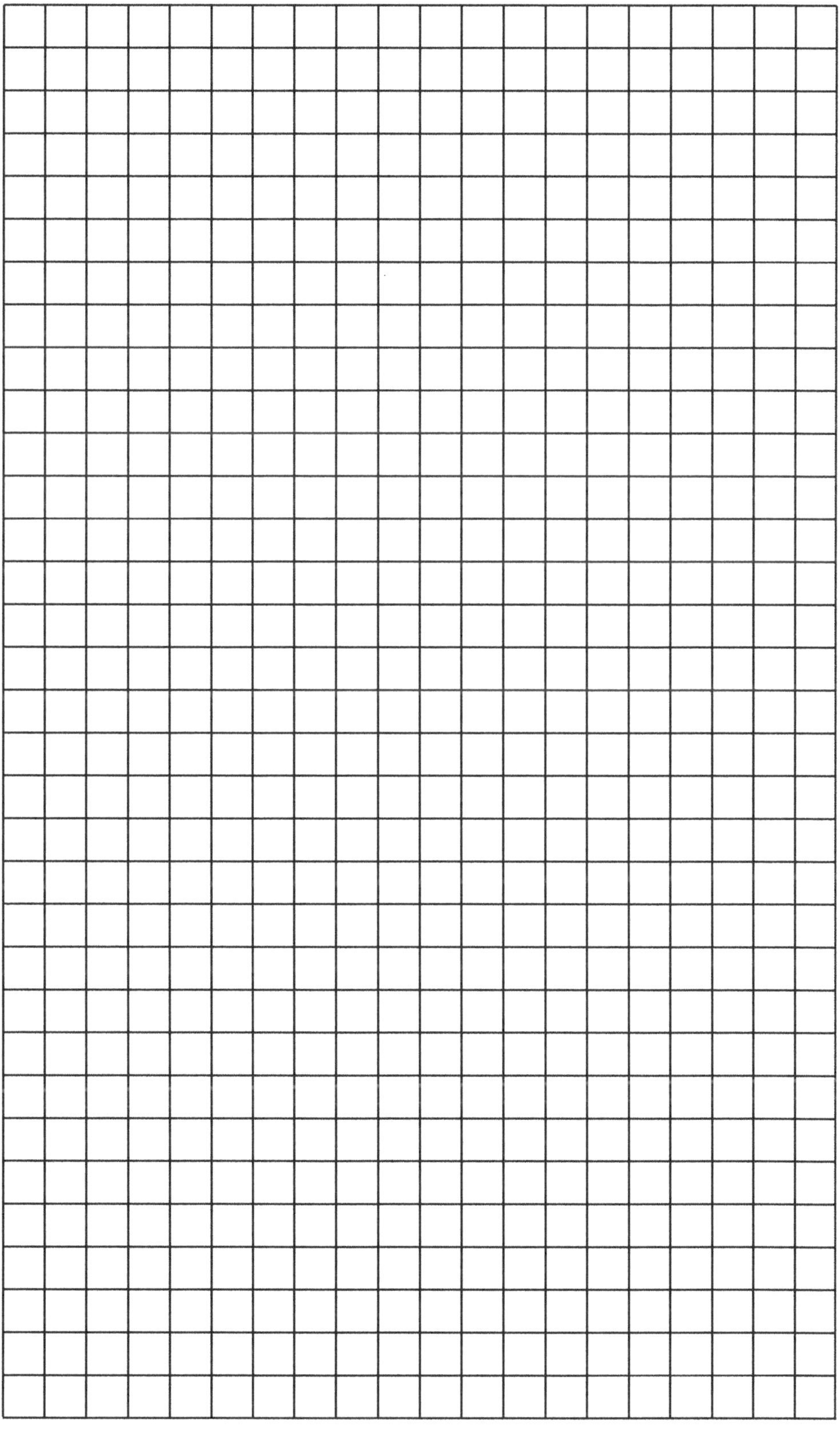

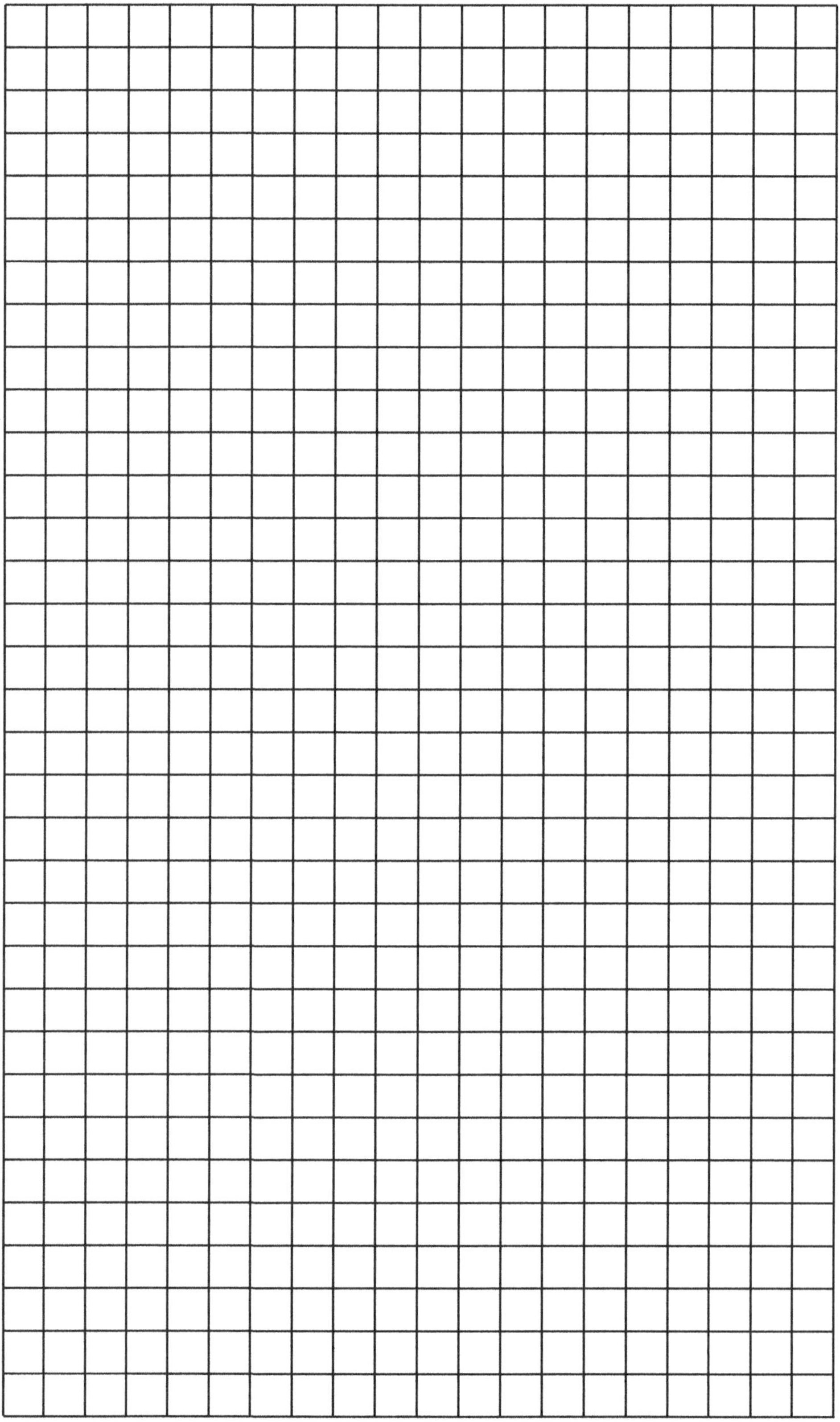

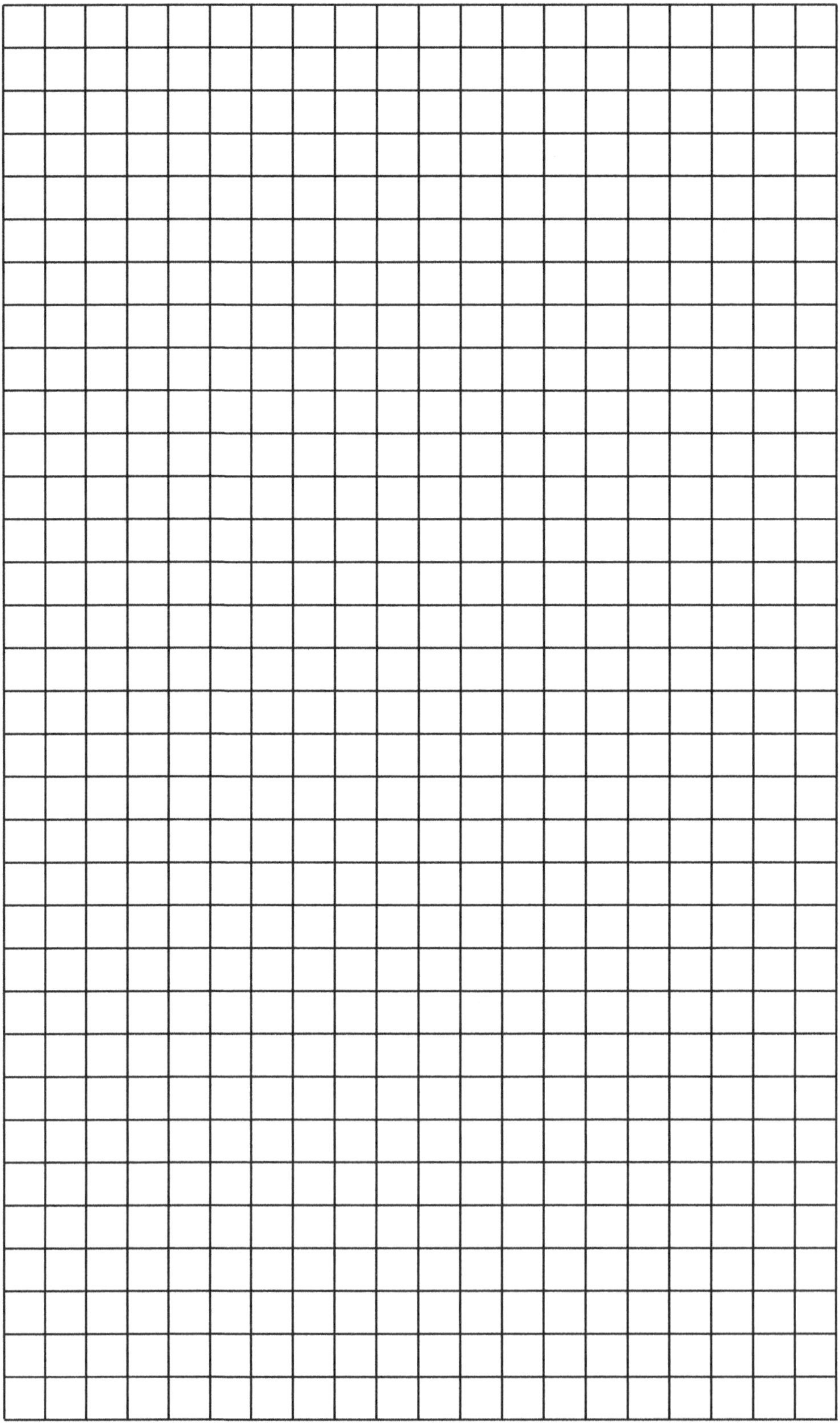

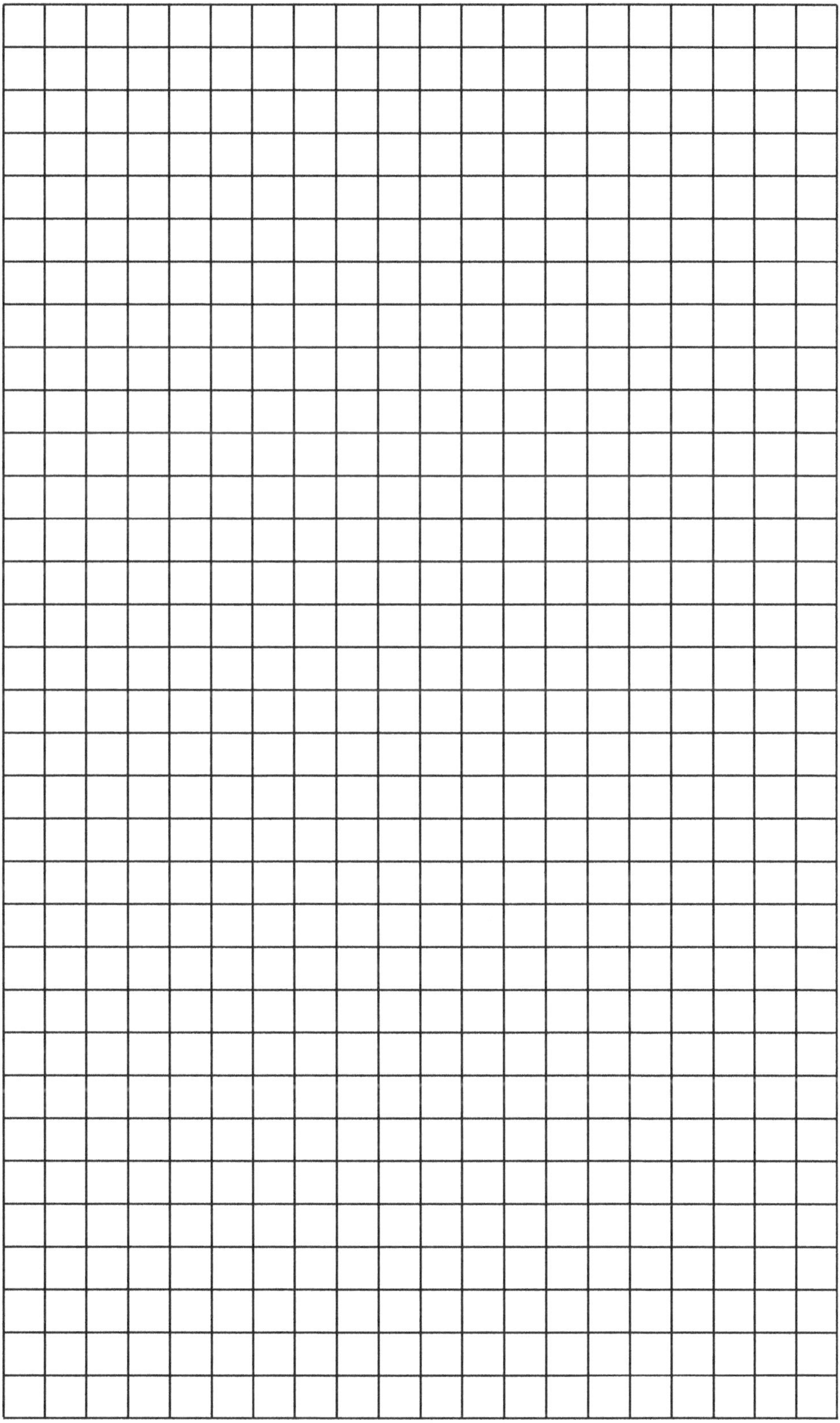

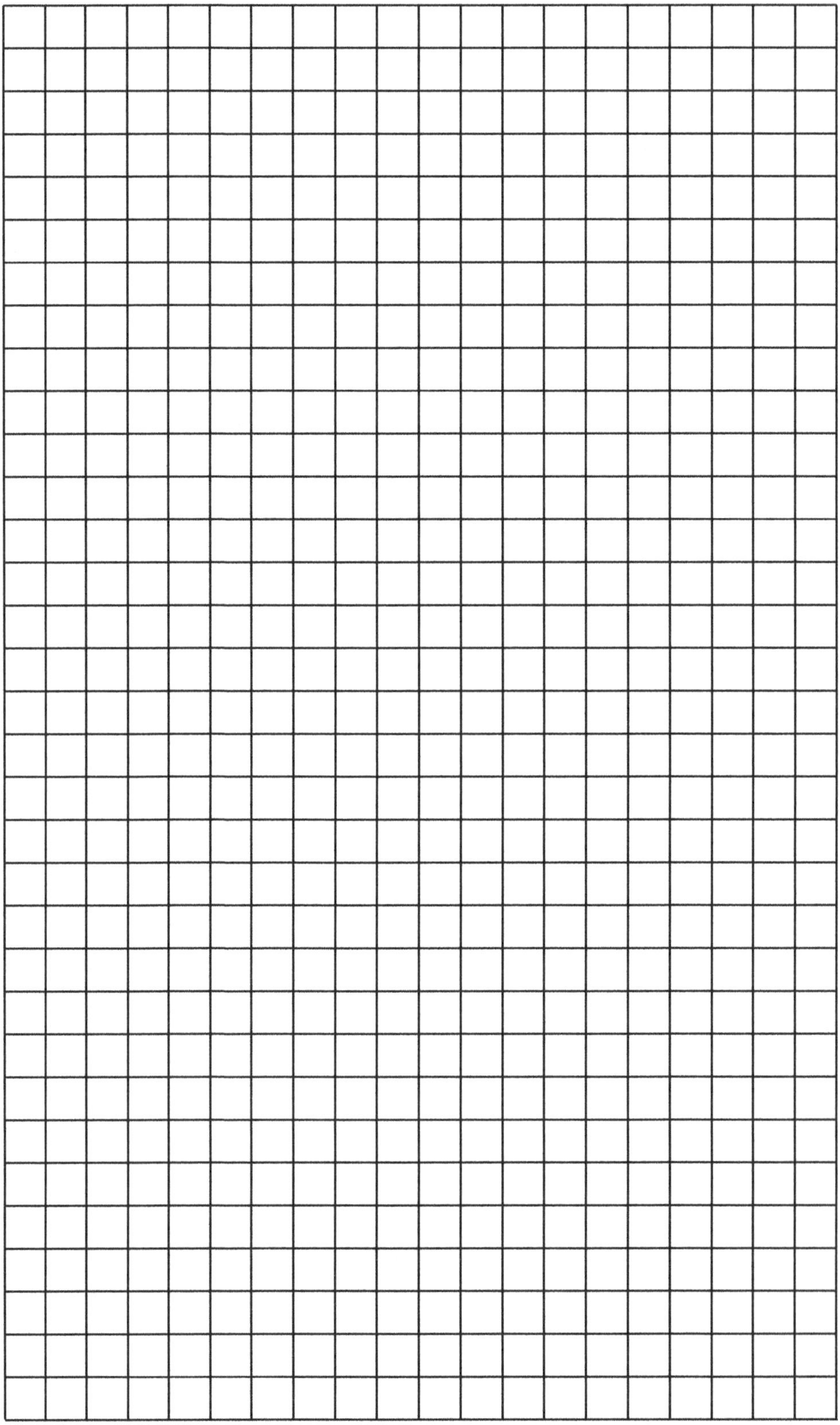

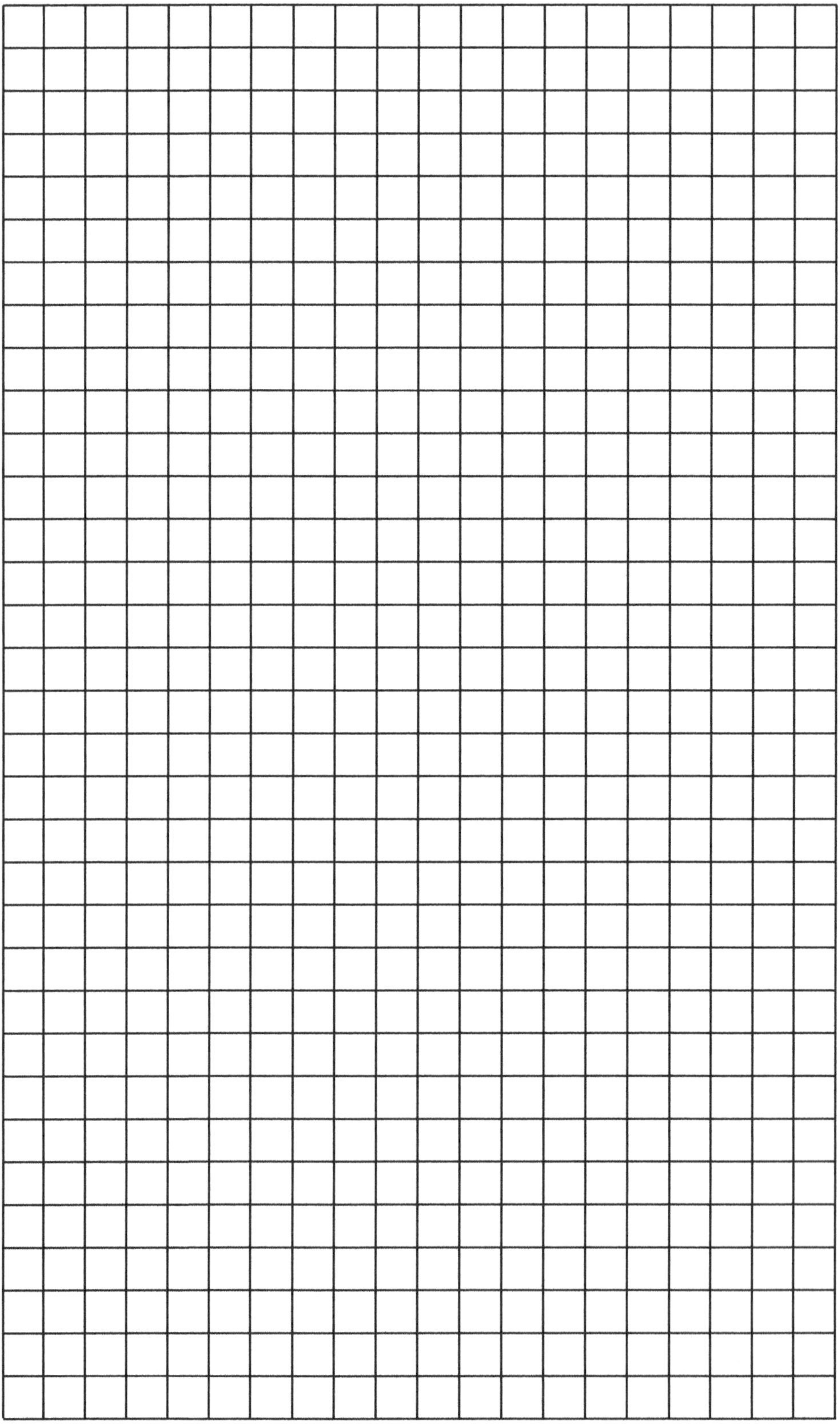

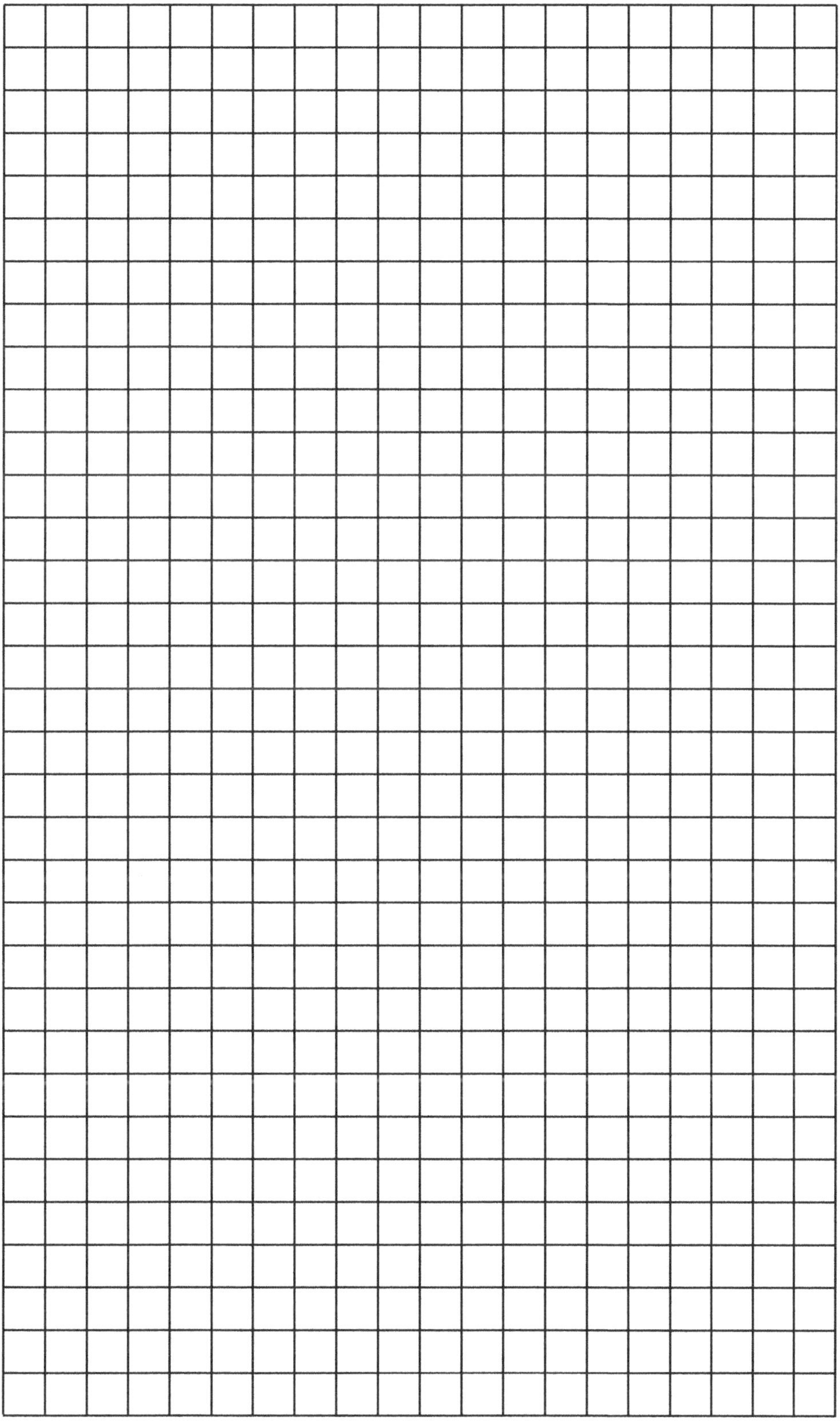

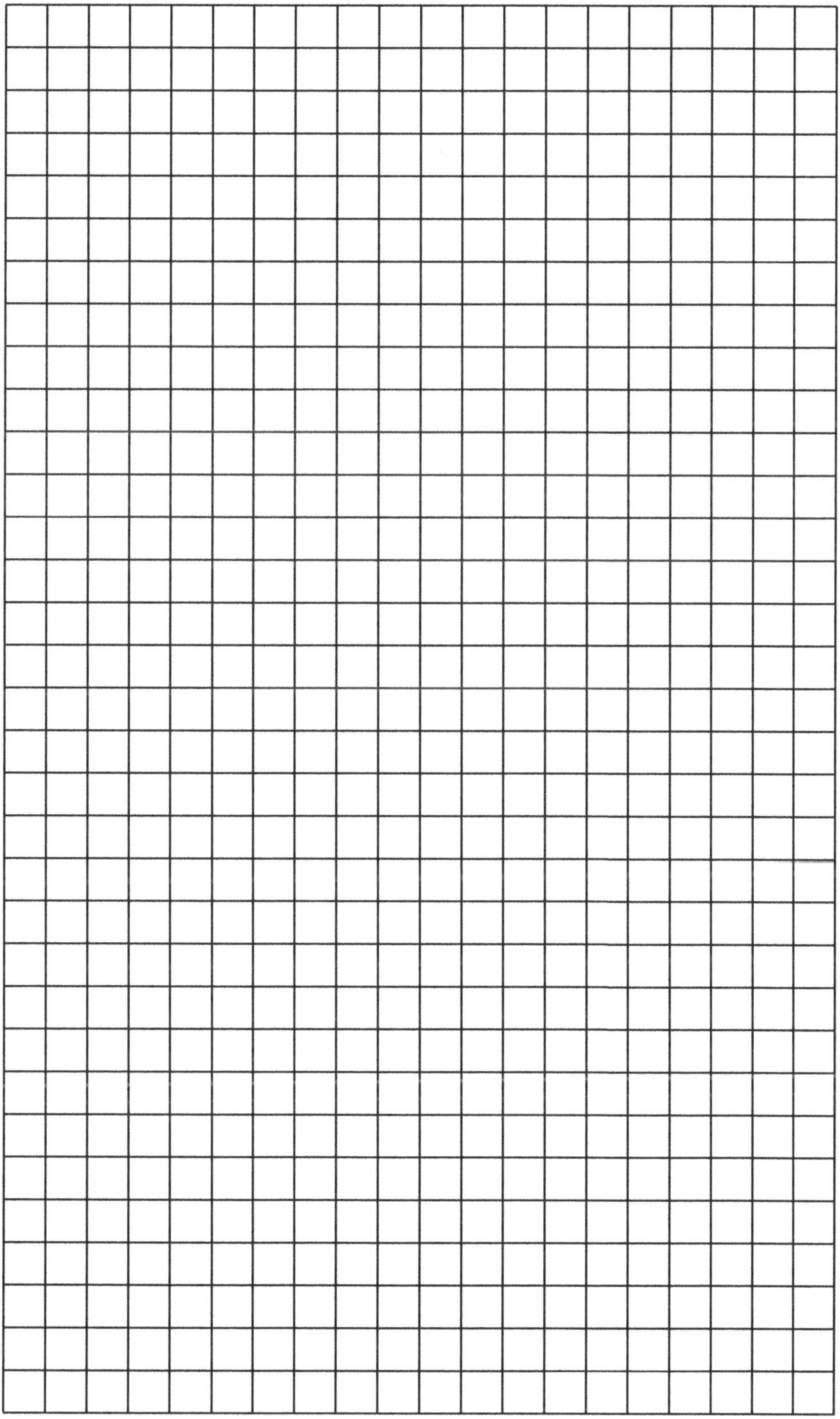

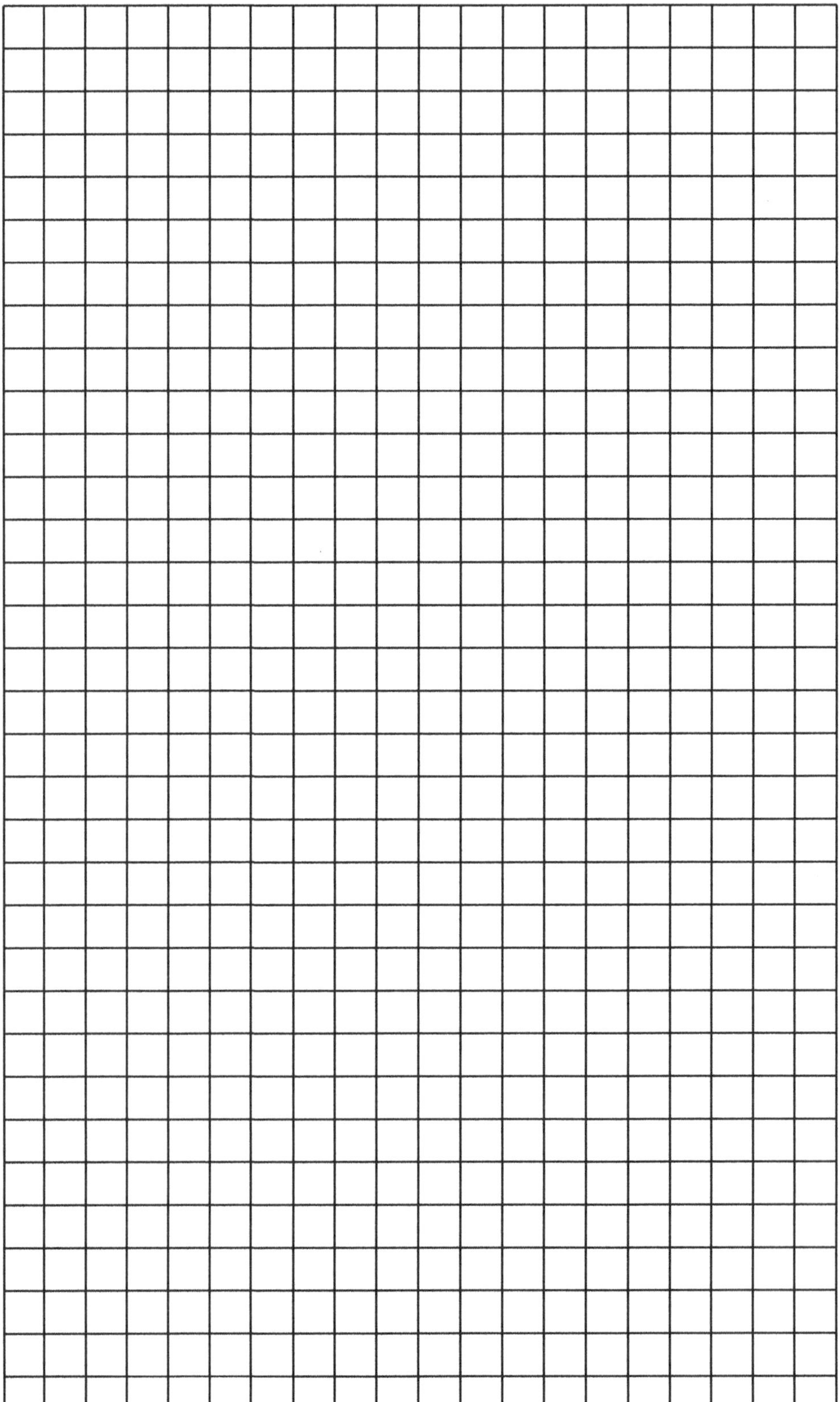

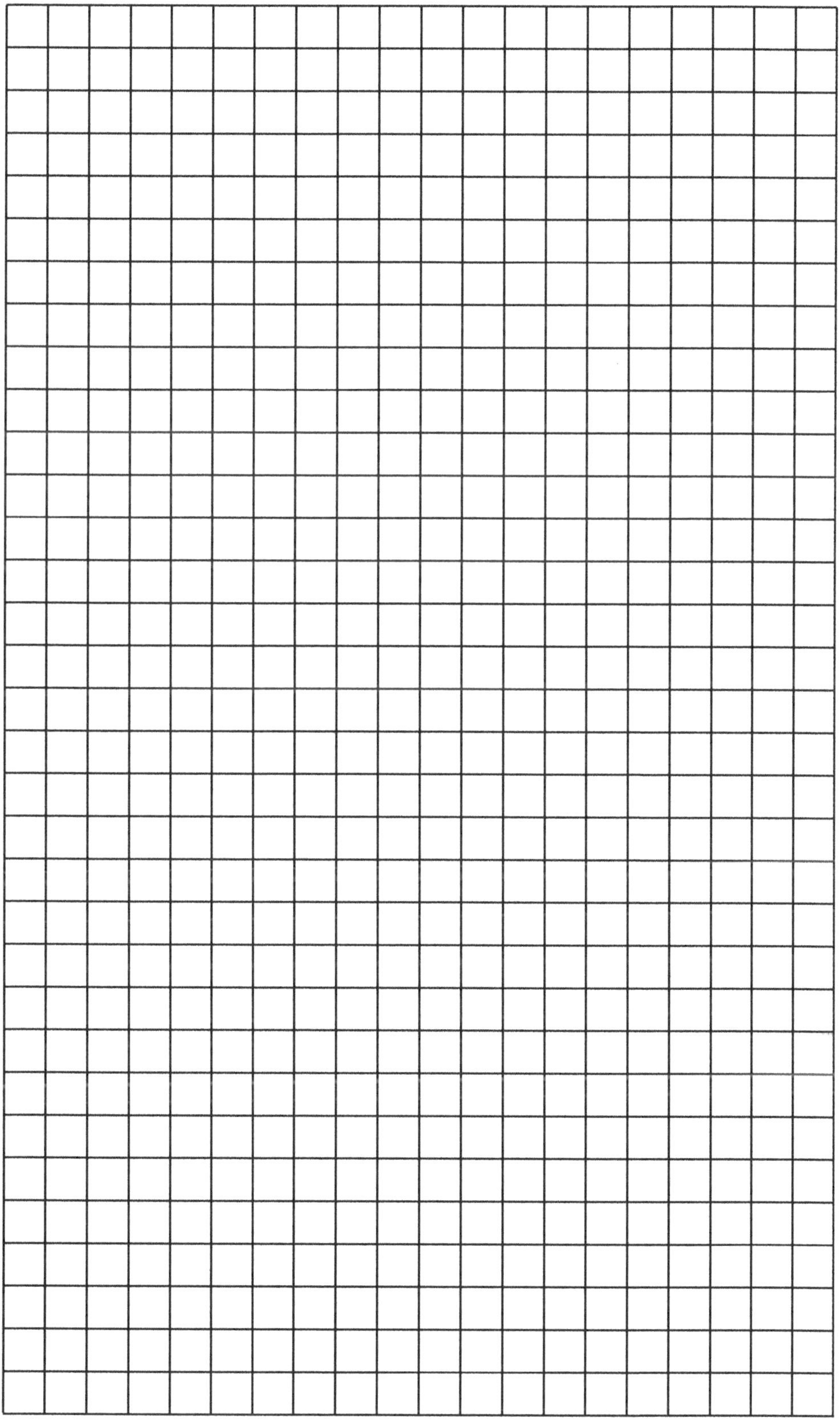

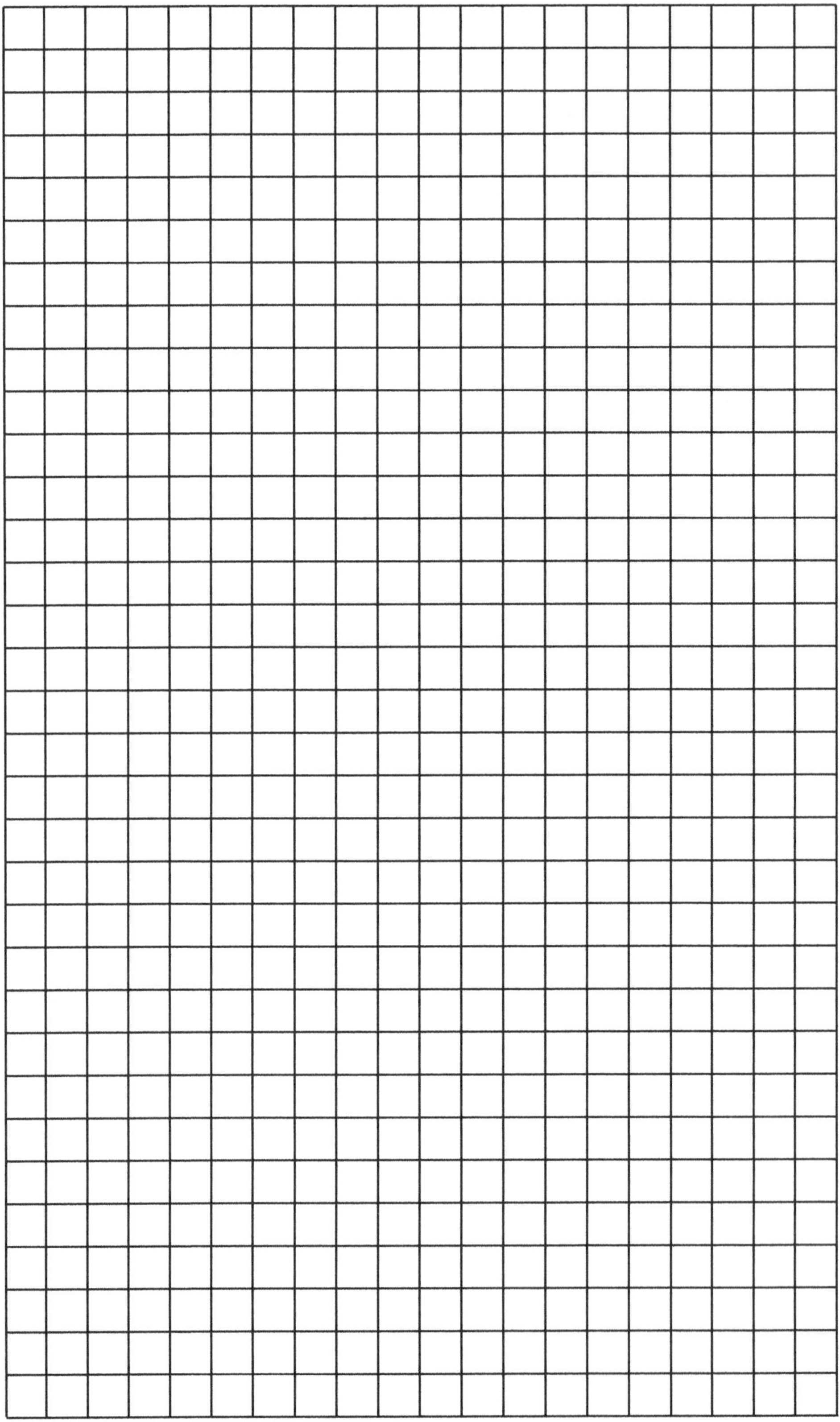

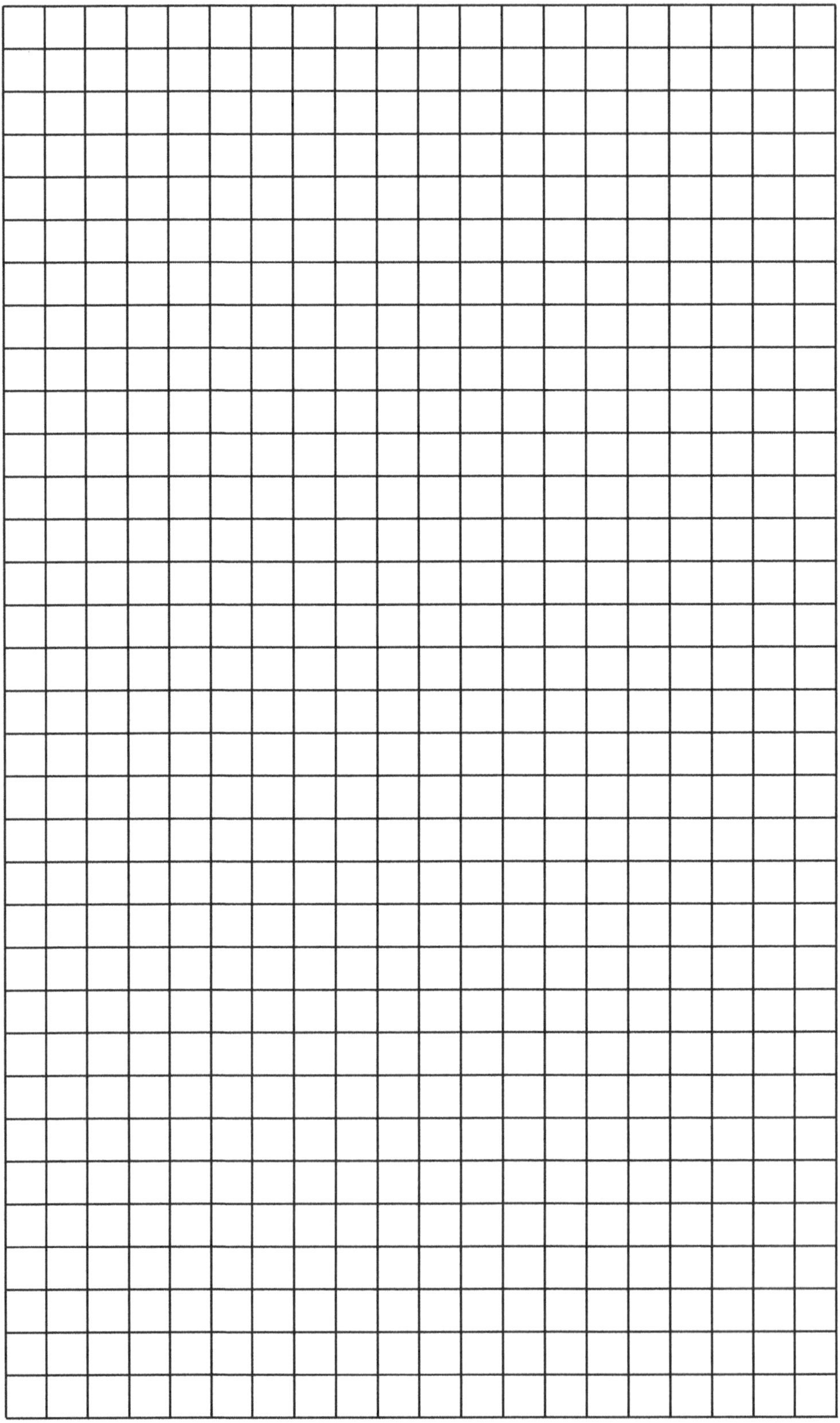

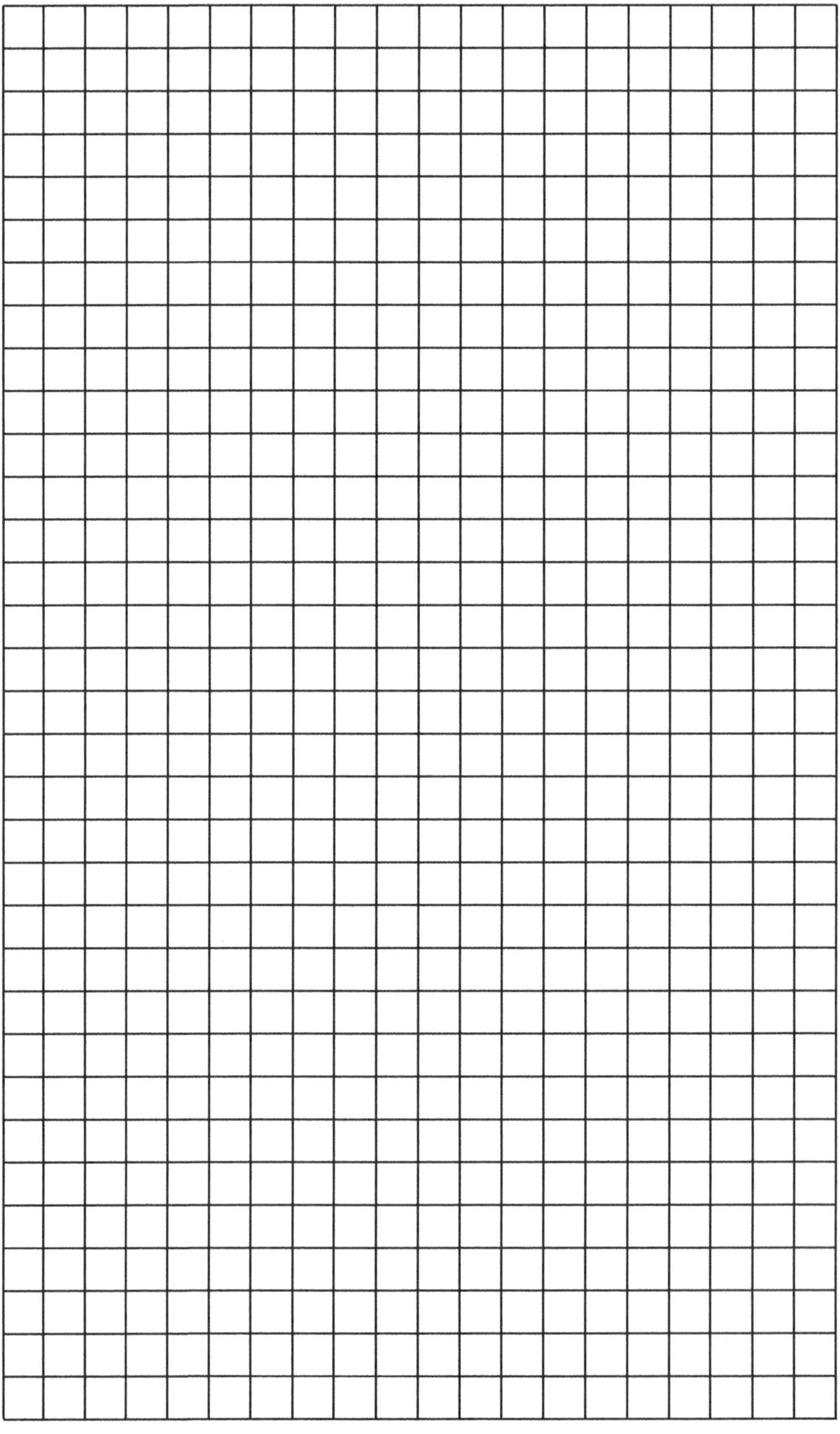

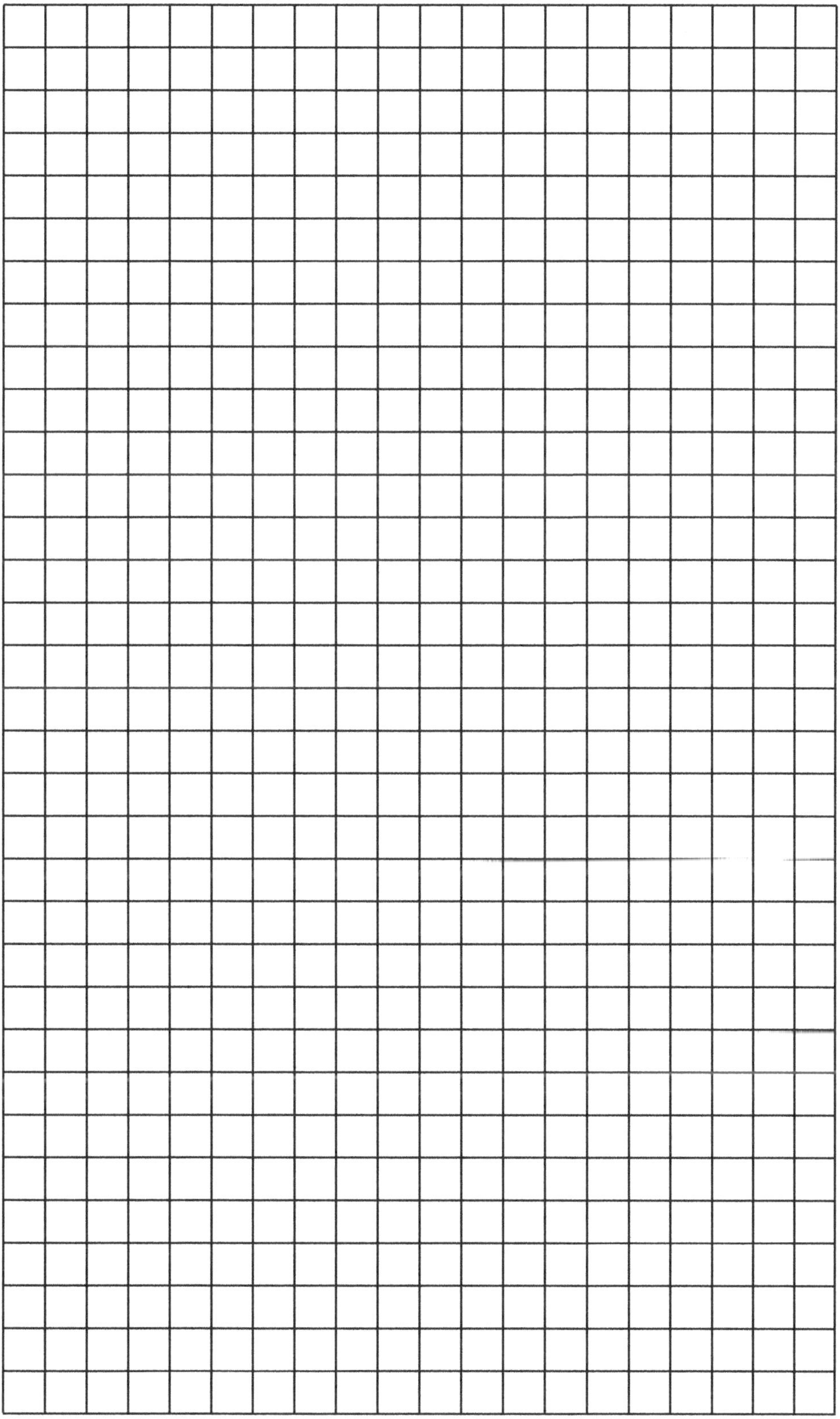

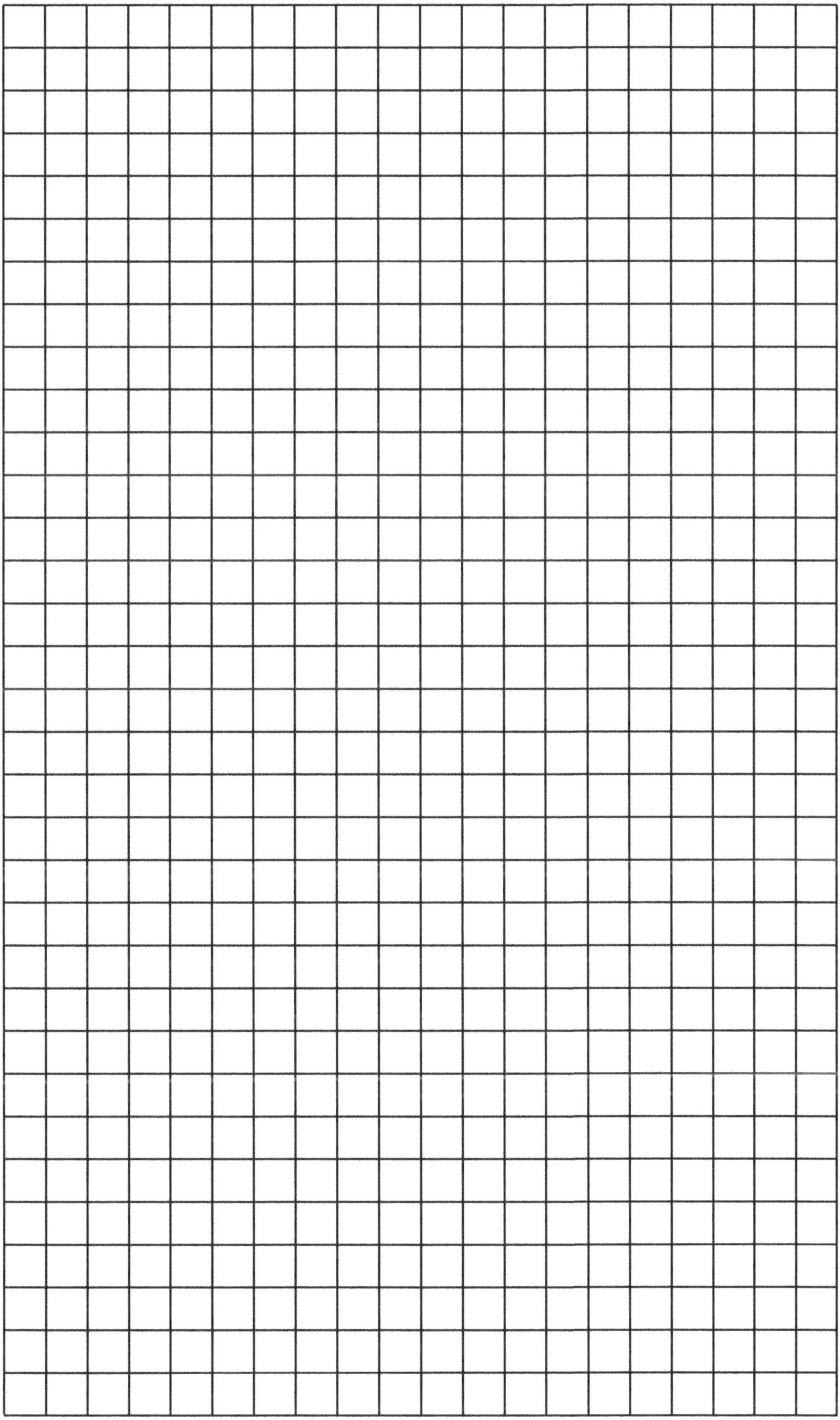

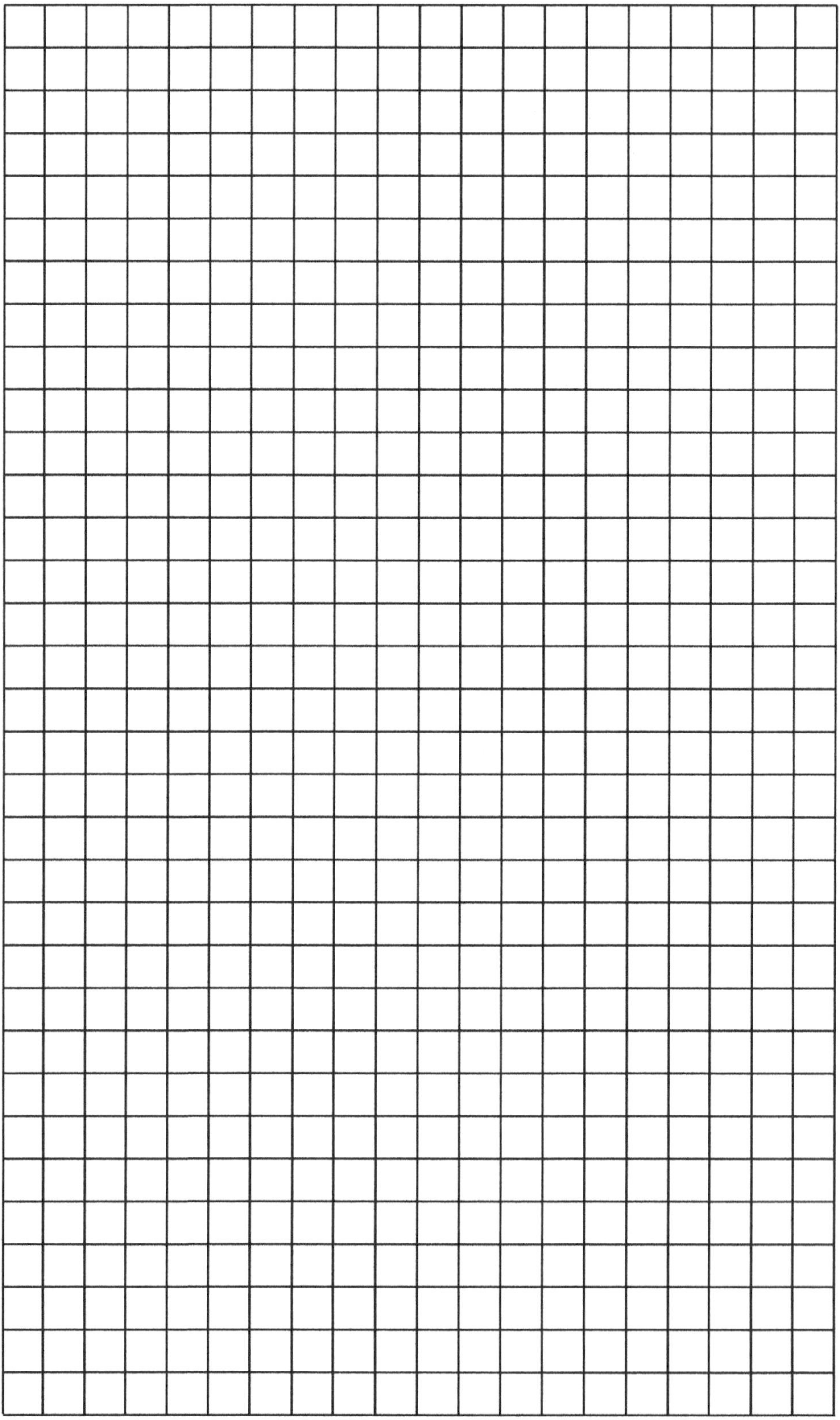

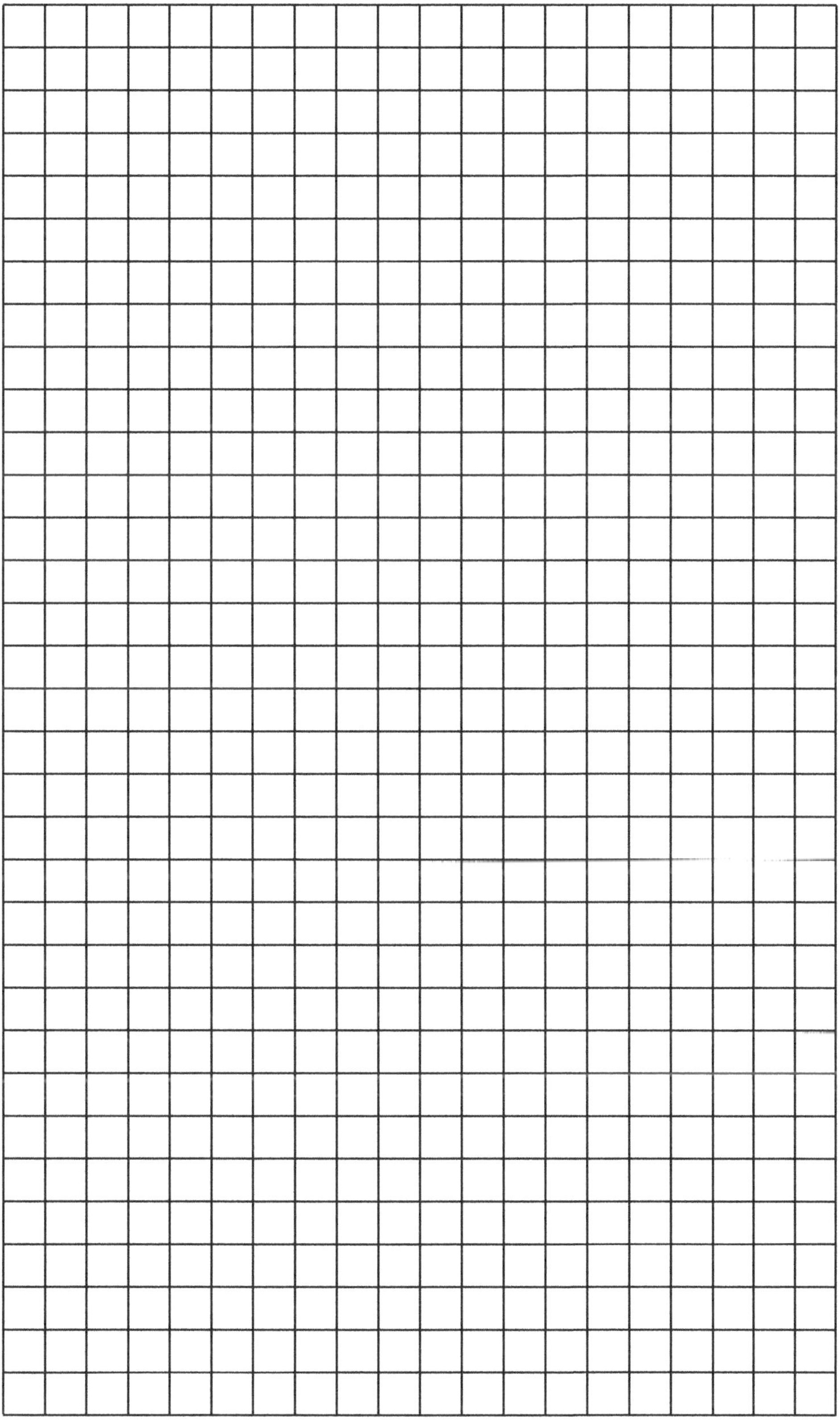

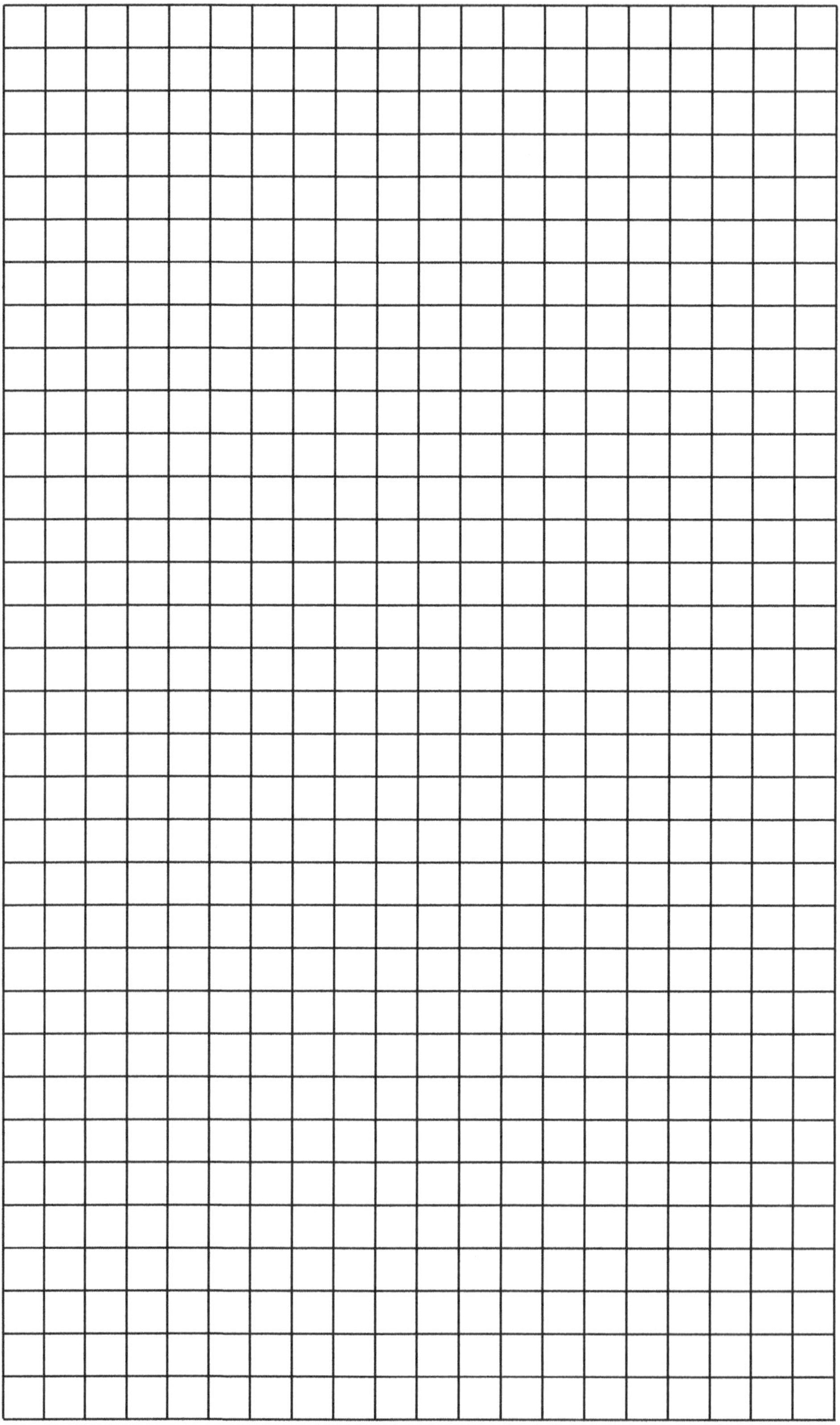

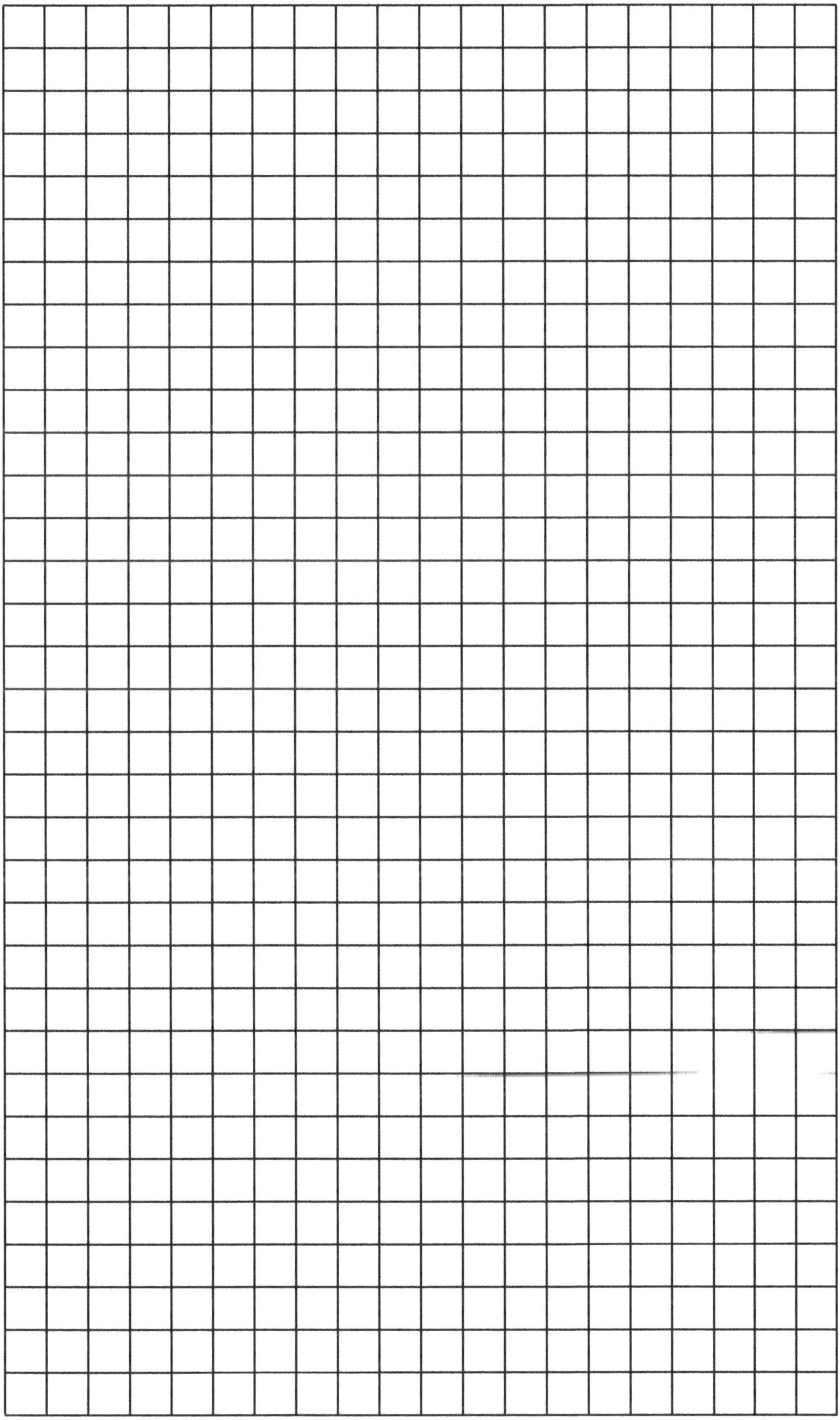

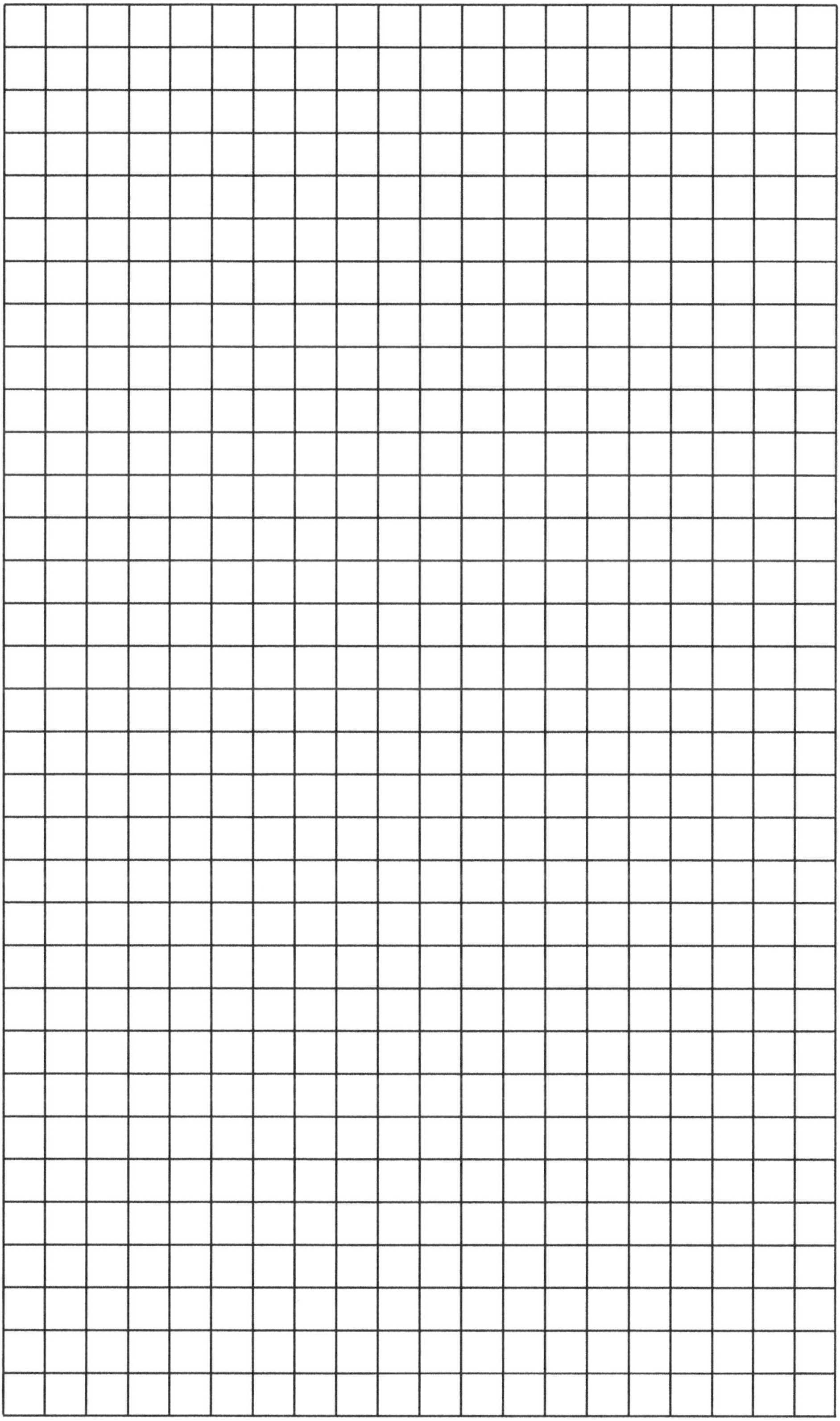

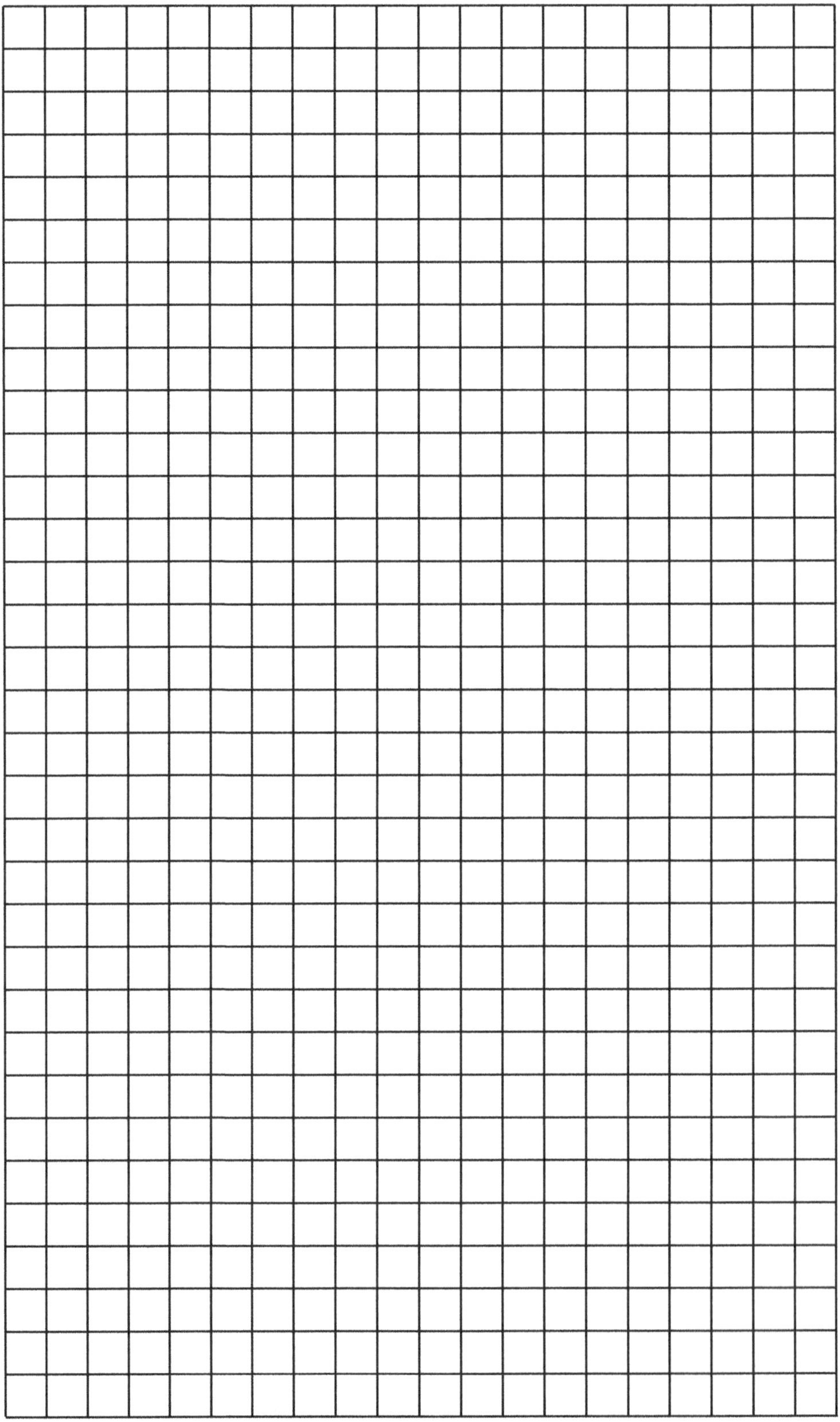

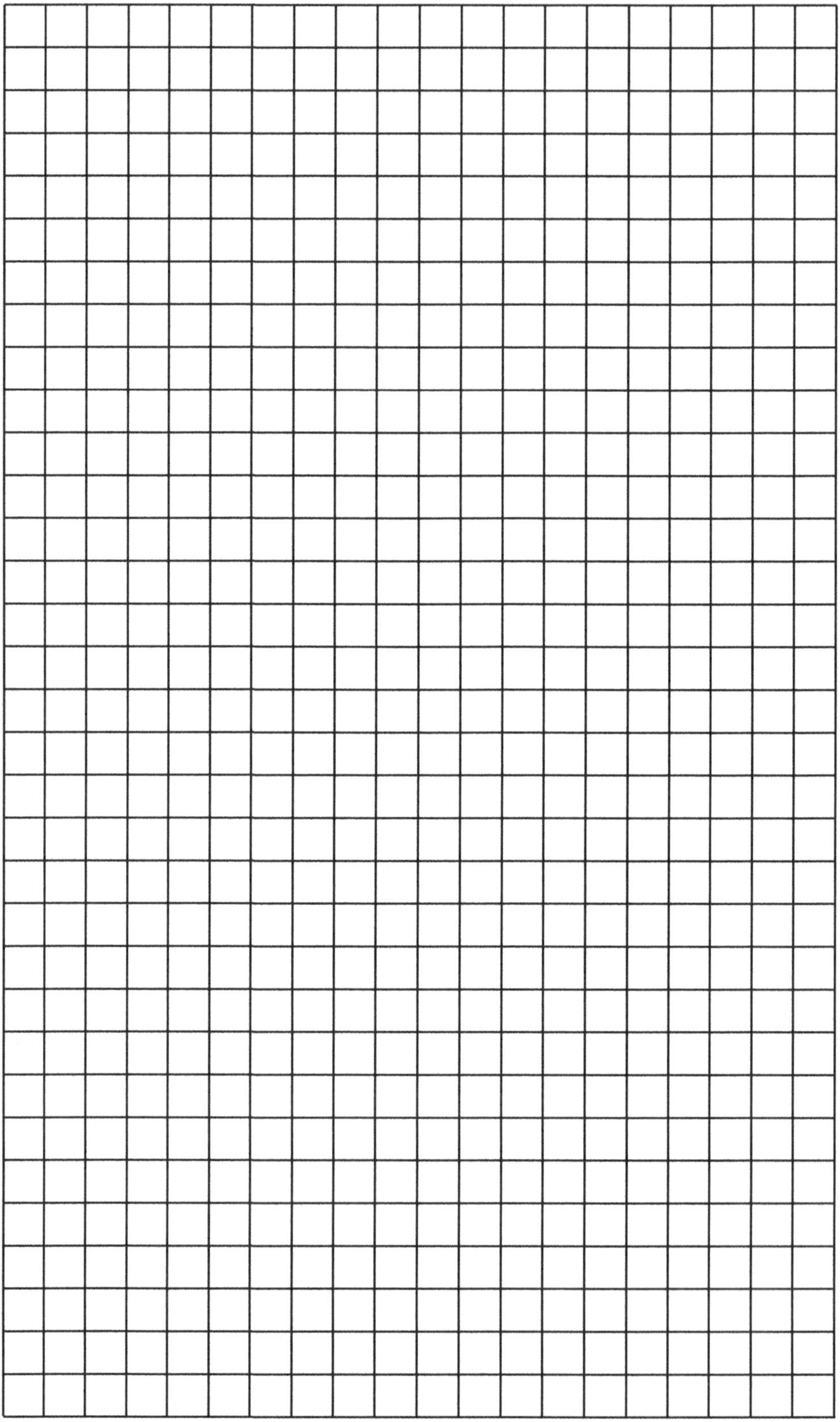

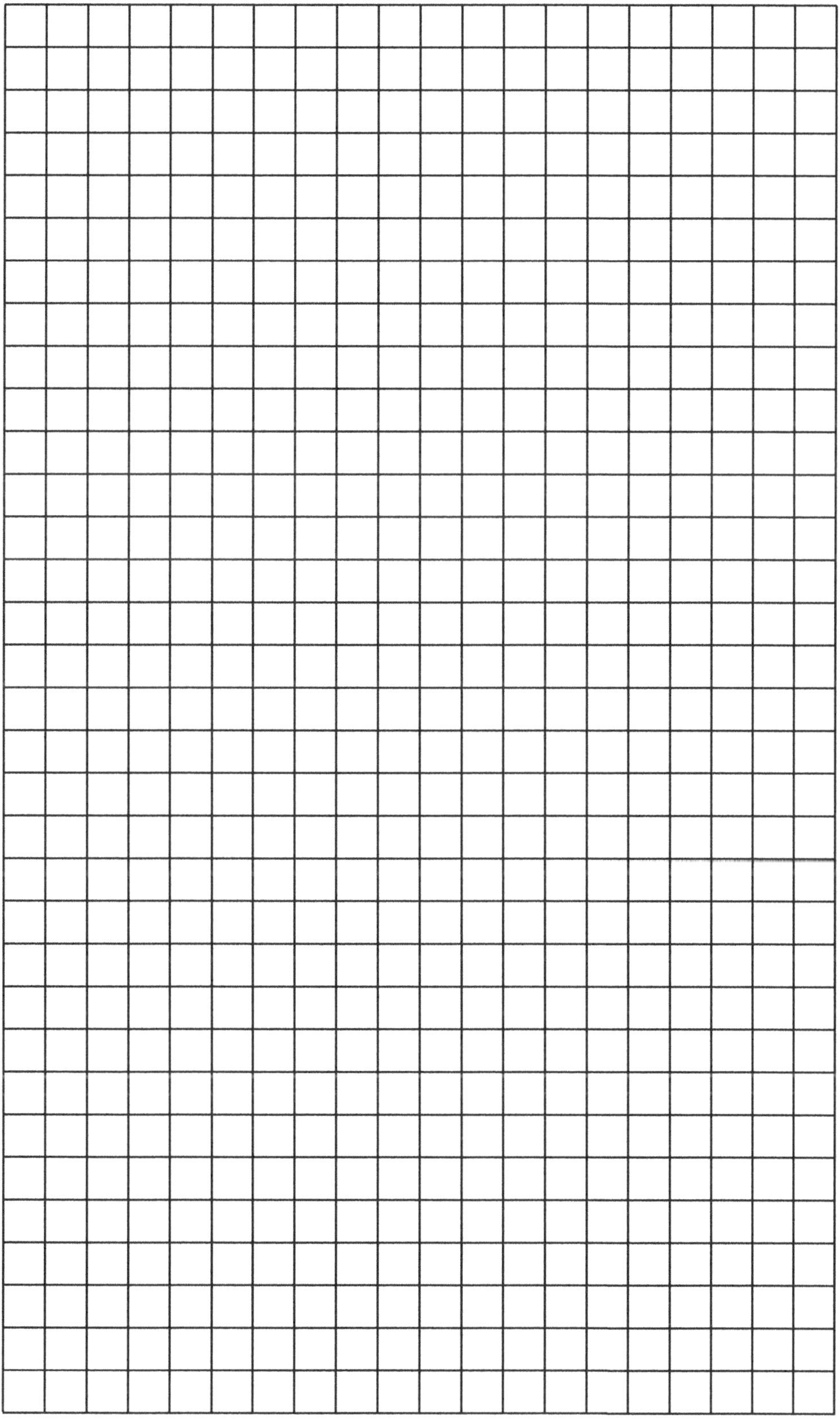

Made in United States
Orlando, FL
11 September 2022

22295523R00065